Affiliate Marketing

How to Make $10,000+ Per Month With Your Own Online Business

Ryan Cash

Contents

Easy Affiliate Marketing...1

The Challenges of Affiliate Marketing 5

Choosing Profitable Products 11

How to Choose the Most Profitable Products...........................14

Writing Reviews..26

Creating a Review Site 33

Scaling Up Your Business...39

Emails..44

Buying Clicks 49

Blog Promotions 52

Avoid These Mistakes...55

Conclusion 59

Easy Affiliate Marketing

What Exactly is Affiliate Marketing?

Affiliate marketing means accepting commissions when you help other businesses and marketers sell their products. If someone buys an item or service through a link you provide, you will be paid a commission from each sale.

This is a very low cost business that can quickly provide a gigantic profit. We will go into much more detail soon of course, but for now, imagine this: You don't need to create any product or service. You don't need to invest much, if anything, to promote affiliate links. And then when someone makes a purchase on your link you immediately get hundreds to thousands of dollars deposited into your account!

What will you do with the thousands of dollars you earn? While you are busy fantasizing about how your will spend this cash, you maybe worrying if it's possible for you to actually succeed. But don't worry. I will tell you exactly how to promote and convince potential buyers to not only click on your affiliate links, but also make multiple, recurring purchases that continually pay you commissions

Anyone can now become a successful online entrepreneur. Affiliate marketing is one of the easiest methods for doing that. Easy doesn't mean effortless of course. You still need to spend some time researching the best affiliate links to promote and figuring out the best promotional practices. We will cover all of that in this book.

There are many techniques for ensuring your success in affiliate marketing. This book will focus on techniques I have personally found effective and used to earn thousands of dollars in affiliate income every month.

I made a lot of mistakes when I first started affiliate marketing. I advertised in the wrong places, wrote substandard sales copy, and chose products that just didn't sell well. Over nearly a decade of trial and error, I've figured out exactly how to profit with affiliate marketing so that my product vendors are happy as we are both earning plenty of cash. This is the book on affiliate marketing I wish I had when I first started earning money online.

I wish I knew all the things I know now so I could have been earning thousands each month immediately instead of after a year of just messing around. I'm very passionate about helping people earn passive income. I know life can be hard and I hope to help make your life a little easier.

The Challenges of Affiliate Marketing

If you are still skeptical about how easy this actually is, then I would like to be honest with you about all the challenges involved in affiliate marketing. This is so that you understand what you will need to overcome to succeed.

Affiliate marketing is a major component of online business. Nearly every online store will now have an affiliate marketing program that you could join. It can be difficult to choose exactly which products and services you want to promote.

Vendors really appreciate your help promoting their products. They don't have to pay for the promotion and they can still get sales. Some vendors even have affiliate competitions in which you get huge bonuses for selling the most.

Customers should also appreciate receiving a product or service they've been looking for. Hopefully you've chosen to promote something of high quality and you are helping people find the exact resources they want.

A great way to promote affiliate links is to create a product review site. On this site you write product reviews including the affiliate link. You can discuss all the features, pros, and cons of the product or service. This helps people decide if they are interested in the product or not.

Some affiliate programs will provide you a bonus to give to customers when they use your links.

When you devote the time and effort to promote affiliate links correctly this can be very profitable.

The Challenges:

We talked about the benefits of affiliate marketing programs. Now lets discuss some challenges.

It may be tempting to lie about products in order to promote them. False advertising stinks. I'm sure you've been to sites trying to sell you on a product but you can't tell if they can actually deliver on all the promises.

It can be difficult for vendors to control all the advertising efforts of affiliate marketers.

Some affiliates will overexaggerate features and lie in the hopes of making sales.

However, most people are savvy and smart enough to smell the inauthenticity of this approach.

So it's very risky and you need to be careful if you ever choose to lie about an affiliate product you are promoting.

It can cause problems for both the vendor and yourself if false promises lead to lots of refunds.

Another challenge I have to mention is that occasionally you may encounter a dishonest vendor who has you promote their affiliate link, but doesn't actually pay you when sales are made.

This seems to be rare in my experience though. I will teach you how to avoid such situations and find trustable vendors.

Even though this is a very lucrative type of business, there are still some risks and challenges you should be aware of.

Affiliate marketing is much easier than many other profitable skills you could learn.

Instead of spending months or years learning how to create a valuable product on your own, instead you only need to learn a few simple marketing techniques that get valuable products in front of potential customers.

You don't have to be a genius to figure out these techniques. The most challenging part will probably be figuring out how to set up a mailing list if you've never done that before.

I know from experience that learning to use a new software can be intimidating at first. However, mailing list services are very easy to figure out. If you ever have any trouble there are also plenty of free online tutorial videos that show you exactly how to do whatever you are trying to do.

The other challenge will be trial and error. You might not make a fortune the first time you promote an affiliate product. However, it's important you don't give up. Treat it as a learning experience. Figure out what you can do better and try again.

Choosing Profitable Products

It's important to choose the right products. You could provide affiliate links for many products and hope you get enough clicks and sales. That's the shotgun approach. By creating lots of content with your affiliate links you will eventually get some sales, but it can be time consuming to search for and set up affiliate promotions for so many products.

The other approach is to choose only several awesome, high quality products that you know for certain sell well. Once you have these chosen you should focus on creating effective promotions that get your affiliate links in front of exactly the people who would buy it.

You don't need to promote hundreds or even dozens of products to make a profit.

In fact if you know how to promote just one product well you could be earning thousands of dollars from that one product alone. You don't need to waste your valuable time writing over exaggerated reviews for lots of products you know nothing about.

The shotgun approach can be tempting, but by devoting more energy in promoting just a few high paying products you are much more likely to make sales commissions.

For high earnings you need to determine which products will be the most worth your time.

New products are launched every day.

There are always more opportunities. It may take some trial and error to find the best products to promote, but if you choose smartly, it won't take long to find exactly what you are looking for.

How to Choose the Most Profitable Products

There are some important factors to consider when choosing affiliate products. When affiliate marketing online first started, most vendors only offered very low commissions. Such as 5 to 20%! That's not much at all. Now, the norm is to offer commissions of at least 50%. So make sure you choose products that offer at least 50% commission if you want to profit.

The exception is when it's a very expensive product or service. In that case, a 30% commission on a 1000 dollar product can earn you 300 dollars per sale. So you would only need to make a few sales to start earning thousands of dollars yourself. If you are worried about finding people who actually have the disposable income to spend on whatever product you are promoting, then don't worry. In a later chapter I will show you how to find exactly the people who will purchase whatever you are selling.

However, very expensive products can still be challenging to sell as the conversion rate is much lower.

Cheaper products can easily sell to hundreds of customers a month. If you sell a $40 dollar product, with a 50% commission you only need to sell to 50 customers to make $1000! That isn't so difficult. You only need to sell that cheap product to 500 customers to earn $10,000. That is exactly what I did, and what I want to teach you to do!

500 customers isn't very difficult at all. Especially when you know how to get your affiliate link in front of thousands of potential new customers every month!

Now, let's compare some of the different products you might be selling.

Digital products:

Digital products include software, eBooks, Online Courses, Audio files, and website memberships.

Digital products are much easier to sell than physical products. Often, people have some problem they want a solution for immediately and an eBook or online course offers exactly what they are looking for, when they want it.

Digital products are great because customers can immediately download or access their purchases. There are billions of dollars being made in digital products every year and you don't even need to exercise your own creativity to profit from them.

Vendors develop their digital products and hope people who need what they are selling will find it. You can help these creative people share their valuable content and earn money at the same time.

Judging Quality

Research every product thoroughly before deciding to promote it. Look at what other people say about it. Chances are you will come across ads and reviewers of people who are trying to promote their own affiliate links. Observe how they are promoting it, but also be aware of any possible over exaggerated promises.

Here are some questions you should ask before deciding on a product:

Is the product something you would buy yourself?

Do you see any weak points in the product's sales page?

Does anything on the sales page make you not trust the vendor?

How persuasive is the sales copy to you?

How well is it selling already?

Can you verify its quality?

It's important to vet every product and make certain it is worth your time to promote. Promoting poor products will just waste your time and ruin your reputation. People won't trust anything you recommend because you've suggested something clearly worthless to them.

Therefore it's important to always choose high quality products that sell well and actually provide massive value to people's lives.

So how do you verify exactly what is in a digital product? There are several methods.

First, you could buy the product yourself. But there is a better way.

Ask.

Just ask the vendor for a "review copy" of their digital product. You can explain that you have a blog, mailing list, or video channel where you review products similar to theirs. Let them know you want to become an affiliate and ask for a review copy of their product to write a review on.

Usually they will send it to you, or give you access to their membership site completely free! Because they are happy someone wants to help them promote their products and services.

You can receive some awesome content this way. Once however, a vendor sent me an E-book that was filled with spelling mistakes and poor writing on every page. Instead of writing a negative review, I told the vendor about the issues and looked for a better product. If you receive products that obviously have lots of flaws, then make sure you don't promote them.

If you aren't able to get a free review copy, it is still possible to create a review and recommendation based on the comments and reviews of other people who have used the product. Also, you can check out how other affiliates are promoting it. Never plagiarize their sales copy of course, but basically you can figure out how to similarly highlight the product's features based on what they've written.

It's also important to choose a product that people actually buy. A good affiliate marketplace site will show you statistics on how well the product is selling. Clickbank.com is one of the best resources you can use to find affiliate programs. They also show you how popular each product is which is very helpful in deciding.

It also pays to do your research. Join some affiliate communities in forums or other social media groups. Observe what products other affiliates are having success with.

You can also go to affiliate Meetups and network with others who are already making lots of money from affiliate links. With a bit of research you can quickly determine which products are best sellers.

Scrutinize the Sales Copy

A good product has an awesome sales page.

Some things you should look for in an awesome sales page:

- filled with details on exactly how the product will solve the customer's problems.
- Convincing social proof and reviews of previous customers
- The price
- Easy and convenient purchasing methods. Such as with PayPal or credit card.

You need to judge the sales copy on your own criteria too. If you read anything that makes you feel sleazy or dishonest then it's probably not going to convince many people. I'm always amazed at how many poorly written sales pages I've read while looking for affiliate programs to promote.

Maybe the products were very high quality, but nobody would ever know because the vendor never took the time to write or hire someone to write convincing sales copy. Or maybe their sales page is just ugly and too simple. If the vendor doesn't make enough money from their product to pay a web designer a few bucks to make a better page, then why would anyone buy the product? Ugly sales pages ruin sales. So be careful.

The sales letter should clearly explain all the features of the product. It should have convincing testimonials, and should feel like it's written by a normal person just trying to share some value with you; not by a marketer trying to trick you into handing over your cash.

You can also do some informal research by asking friends, family and online group members what they think of the sales copy. If most people you ask would buy the product if needed then it's probably a good choice.

What to Promote

The great thing about many affiliate programs is that they already provide you with all the promotional content you need to make money with their products!

This includes:

- Ads of every size
- Banners
- Articles
- Sometimes video and audio samples
- Ebooks
- Emails
- And other content

You usually don't even need to spend time creating ads and reviews because they've already done that for you. You just choose the appropriate sized ad you want to use and can sign up for advertising services like AdSense and Facebook ads.

Or, you choose an email template you want to send your email list including your affiliate link. You don't even need to write anything if you don't want to. All the tools you need are already available.

Upselling

If you aren't familiar with this term it means selling more products to a customer after they've made the initial purchase. For example, a customer buys a product and you get your commission and the customer is added to the vendor's email list.

Then if the customer makes more purchases of the vendor's other items, you can get another commission from that additional sale too.

In marketing terms, this is also known as a sales funnel.

A customer has already invested in product A so is more likely to invest in product B.

You can also receive commissions on recurring payments when customers sign up for membership services.

Though this type of commission is less common, it's nice to have a regular income from this type of product.

No matter what types of products you sell, always make sure it is a quality product that sells well and has a low refund rate. You now have a solid understanding of how to vet your products and ensure you choose something people will buy.

Writing Reviews

We will talk more about where to post your reviews in later chapters. In this chapter we will discuss how to write quality reviews that convert into sales.

This is an important skill. Poorly crafted reviews lose potential customers as they lose interest in your message and click away.

Customers compare products before a purchase so it's important to share any important information that could be a deciding factor in purchasing.

If you can get a review copy of the product then evaluate it thoroughly. Write an article that talks about all the pros and cons of the product.

If you are still confused about how to write a review copy request to a potential vendor, then here is an example:

Hi (Vendor's name)

I'm (your name). I'm very interested in joining your affiliate program for (Vendor's product). Is it possible to get a review copy of (product) in order to write a review which I will post on (My review site, blog, facebook ad, etc.)?

Thanks for your time!

(your name)

As you can see, it doesn't take much to convince a vendor to provide you with a copy of their product so you can help them make money. However, it does help to show you have a site or at the very least a social media group where you will be posting the review. If you want, you can also explain a little of your marketing plan for the product.

If the vendor isn't willing or capable of offering a free copy, then you can ask for at least a discount.

If that is still not possible and you are convinced this is a high quality best seller, then you can consider actually purchasing the item to craft an honest review.

Often, vendors I've never worked with before will suddenly send me emails offering me free products or services in exchange for posting affiliate linked reviews. If your review site is in a specific niche, this can easily happen to you too.

It's important to write your review well because good reviews equal good sales.

You don't need to write really long reviews. Only 300 to 500 words should be enough. Any more and it's possible to bore potential customers. You don't need to oversell the product. That's the vendor's job. You're only job is to make potential customers curious enough to click your affiliate link. If your vendor has a great sales page then that should convert these customers into sales and of course commissions for you.

Keep your reviews on point. Only include the most important information. Also edit the review several times. Make sure you carefully examine every word and see if it is necessary or not.

Share the good and bad about the article. You should find at least one "bad" point or con about product as this feels more authentic. Whenever people read reviews that saw the product is flawless, 5 star, revolutionary and life changing people just don't trust you because that kind of innovation is extremely rare. If you are a normal human being judging a product then you can probably find something about the product that isn't perfect.

If the product has plenty of great features a customer wants they will still buy it. Your "bad" point could be that the content is a little short but the content that is there is very valuable. Or you could say you mentioned a few editing mistakes, but overall the content is of high quality, so you didn't mind, for example.

Write as if you were telling a buddy about a product you recently tried. Again, don't oversell it, just explain your experience with the product. It's also useful to include some testimonial quotes from other users. These can usually be found on the product's sales page. As much as you can, share your honest opinion about it. You don't need to exaggerate in the hopes of getting more sales. Often, an average though honest review converts better than a glowing review that claims a product is flawless. At least in my experience that is.

Be sure to use product photos in your article. Seeing what the product looks like is essential to inspiring their curiosity.

You can also use a rating system in your articles. Such as 5 stars, or 1 to 10. The rating makes it easy for readers to get an idea of your opinion of the product without carefully reading every sentence of your review.

If you can demonstrate yourself using the product, or even better, your results from successfully using the product, then share it in a video.

This adds a lot of credibility and you are sure to get plenty of sales with this social proof.

In the next chapter, you will finally find out where to post all your profitable reviews.

Creating a Review Site

Once you have your review articles ready, where do you put them? The best option is to set up your own website. If you've never done that before, don't worry, you are about to find out how.

Using the blogging platform Wordpress, you can easily set up an impressive website

without even knowing how to code HTML,
CSS and Javascript.

Your Domain Name

First, you'll have to register a domain name. NameCheap.com is one of the cheapest options, though you are of course free to shop around.

On a domain registrar site such as NameCheap.com, you can search for the availability of your desired site names. It's important to use a clear and easily understandable site name.

Many affiliate marketers include the product name in the domain name. This is useful as search engines place priority on sites that have search terms in the domain name. It can be effective, though usually it means it makes more sense for the site to focus on promoting that specific product.

It's also useful to choose a niche and right reviews of several niche specific products. In that case your domain name could be something like:

FitnessBookReviews.com

weightliftingCourses.com

DogTrainingBonuses.com

I've found the most success with domain names that include the word "review."

Take your time to choose between several domain names you like. When you decide on the best available name then register it and it's yours.

Next, you'll need to host your domain name on a server. Sites like Hostgator.com offer domain servers that host all your websites files on their servers. The idea is basically their servers are always connected to the internet, so your site should always be online.

I recommend you shop around for a web host that meets your needs and budget.

By registering your site you get a .com website. This is more trustworthy than affiliate sites with the _____.wordpress.com extension. Dot com websites are taken much more seriously than typical blog sites.

It only costs a few dollars a month to host a website. It is also often cheaper to purchase long term hosting plans.

If you are still not convinced you will make this tiny investment back within a year, then purchase only 3 months of hosting. I guarantee if you follow the steps in this book that you WILL be making sales commissions to cover that minimal investment within that short time.

Once you have your hosting plan, next install Wordpress. It has many free themes that look very professional. There are also some great free themes for Review sites! Choose a theme and adjust the settings to your liking. You can also install some useful plugins for various features. Such as antispam, and SEO article editors for example.

Next, you should add your review articles. For now, one great article will be enough.

Though it's useful to also add a few more articles relevant to the reviewed product.

Scaling Up Your Business

Once you have your affiliate site set up it's time to collect some customers.

Most internet marketers will agree that it's essential to build a mailing list and attract subscribers. But how do you get these subscribers?

There are many ways. The most common is paid traffic. Send potential customers to your affiliate site. Once there, give them a subscription offer, such as a free book, or list of your top 10 favorite mobile apps for ___, or anything you want. In exchange, you get their email.

It's much smarter to send potential customers to your affiliate site rather than directly to the vendor's sales page because then you can build a mailing list!

With this list, you can send subscribers more offers with affiliate links included.

To do this, you must create a landing page.

It must have:

1. No navigation (because they are less likely to click something and get distracted.)
2. A headline
3. A visual of the free offer, such as a book cover
4. An optin form

5. And an obvious download button

The headline should include a call to action that inspires the reader.

Here's an example:

DOWNLOAD THIS FREE REPORT AND LEARN HOW I EFFECTIVELY SAVE TIME WITH THESE 3 APPS!

Writing this large font headline in all caps will also make it more readable.

Next you should include a nice visual to make this report feel more tangible and valuable. You can find some free 3d book cover websites online that can generate these graphics for you.

Next, include an optin form where users can enter their email and a big bright button that says download.

Wordpress has some free options for creating an email list from subscribers, but I've never found it effective.

For one thing, the emails always end up in spam folders.

There are other great options out there such as mailchimp and aweber.

Imnica also offers it's services cheaply at only 5 dollars a month.

Once you chose a mailing list service, you can set up an autoresponder. This is an email that's automatically sent to subscribers of your list.

Once you have all this set up, you are ready to get started.

You'll need to send traffic to your subscription landing page, build an email list, then send links to your affiliate review articles on your site, or even directly to the vendors site.

You will also need to create a download page where subscribers can download your free offer once they give you their email.

Emails

Now that you have a mailing list, you can start sending affiliate offers to the people on your list. You can send them directly to the affiliate vendor's sales page, or to your own review page.

To do that, you need to write an email that explains why they should click on the link provided in the email.

The first thing people see in an email is the subject. In the subject you need to make them interested enough to click. A common technique is to use scarcity. Such as to say it's a "limited time offer," or "Only Available to the first 50 People." Keep the subject as short as possible. Email services usually only show the first 50 characters of the subject. People need to be able to read the entire subject with one quick look.

The content of your message should get right to the point. Explain what benefit they will get from your offer and tell them click the link for more information. Keep it short. At most about 300 words. Longer emails test attention spans.

Add the link to the affiliate vendor and/or your review only 3 times in the email. In the beginning, middle and end. It can also be helpful to link to another free bonus on your website which includes a relevant review or affiliate offer.

There are many different techniques for gaining affiliate sales from email lists. You are free to experiment and find what works for you.

However, I will share a 4 day email sequence I've had a lot of success with.

Day 1: First Promotional Email

Day 2: Reminder Email

Day 3: Limited Time Bonus Offer

Day 4: Last Chance Email

Important: With mailing list service autoresponders you can set up these emails to be sent automatically over 4 consecutive days after subscribers subscribe to your mailing list.

Overtime, you can edit these 4 important emails and observe which changes lead to the most click throughs and sales conversions. You can also try this with A/B Testing. That means in Group A you use one set of emails and in Group B you use another.

The first email introduces your affiliate product and how it can benefit them.

The second reminds them of all the value they could get from taking the offer and reminds them of what they are missing out on or what opportunities they are losing.

The third offers something for free that is easily downloadable from your website. The page on your site will also have a link to the affiliate offer you've been telling them about.

In the fourth you amp up the scarcity and tell them its their last chance to get this great offer from your provided link.

It is possible you could offer a discount to subscribers who use their links to make a purchase. But telling them the discount is about to expire, or the content won't be available to purchase within one week they are more likely to at least click the link to make sure the product could provide value to their lives.

Buying Clicks

Now that you have your website, free offer, and autoresponder emails set up, it's time to collect subscribers.

There are many ways to do this. If you already have an online social media platform with lots of subscribers then this part could be very easy.

However, most normal people just don't care about accumulating meaningless "followers" on social media. The solution is to buy traffic to your site.

Google offers one of the best options for doing this. Their Adwords program allows you to place links to your site, on other sites with similar keywords.

Sign up for google Adwords and create your account now.

Next you will need to choose your keywords and "bid" on them. Different keywords have different costs.

Then, figure out your Adwords budget. Start with a small amount and slowly double it every few days as long as you are still getting enough click throughs and subscribers. It's also useful to choose long keyword phrases. Such as "How to install Wordpress."

Google Adwords allows you to track all the clicks to your site. This way you can figure out how many clicks you are getting and compare the number to how many actually subscribe after clicking through to your site. If less than half are signing up after clicking into your site then it could have some problems. Try editing the content, making everything look more professional and trying different images.

Facebook advertising is also a very effective option. It allows you to specify exactly who you want your site advertised to. You can chose to advertise it to men, women, graduates, people of certain ages, and almost any detail you can think of. That is why Facebook wants people to use real information on its site. So that they can advertise to certain people.

Blog Promotions

Writing blog articles shows that you aren't just an online marketer. It demonstrates you are a human being with real thoughts and opinions too. It lets you build a relationship with subscribers. Everyone is more likely to purchase something from someone they trust.

Write articles about any topic you like. However, try to keep them relevant enough to the products you are selling. Share your opinions as honestly as possible. Show your picture. People are more likely to buy from you when they know what you look like.

It's also helpful to write guest posts for other bloggers in your niche. Many of them accept guest posts as they love having more content on their site. You can easily find these opportunities by searching for "(your niche) guest posts."

At the end of you guest post you will be allowed to provide a link to your site at the end of the post. This allows the established blogger's audience to find your site and subscribe to your content.

Writing a good guest post isn't difficult. Each site will have different standards. Some sites, such as thoughtcatalog.com have many readers but incredibly low standards and anyone can write something for them!

But if you want to create a quality post that will get you more subscribers then I have some tips for you.

Use relevant images. Many bloggers will find images on your own. But it's always convenient for them if you can find appropriate images yourself. It should be high quality and attention grabbing.

Be sure to link to your site as many times as you are allowed to in the blog post. This is usually one or two times.

Avoid These Mistakes

There is a lot of competition in online internet marketing. If you want to be an affiliate for a bestselling product, do a quick search for the product and you'll likely find many other affiliates have already snatched dozens of domain names including the product. It may seem difficult to compete, but there are still many opportunities as long as you know how to do promote products properly.

If you want to succeed, please avoid the following common mistakes:

Junk Mail

This is a mistake everyone should be familiar with. You know you've gotten lots of horrible emails trying to convince you to buy something you didn't even need, so why would you inflict the same thing on someone else?

Sending lots of emails doesn't necessarily mean you are going to make more sales. Only send emails when it's relevant and necessary.

A common way of avoiding this is using double opt-in email lists. This means the subscribers need to give you their email, and then click on a subscription confirmation link within the first email you send them. Since they've already confirmed they want to be added to your list, they shouldn't consider you as spam. Over the next 4 days send them the 4 emails we mentioned earlier and you should see results. Also make sure they can easily unsubscribe if they want to. Whenever a subscriber declares your messages as spam when they can't unsubscribe it can give you problems.

Poorly Written Content

Make sure you write well. Edit your emails thoroughly. Whenever I receive affiliate emails with poor grammar and bad spelling I NEVER click on their links. It just makes me feel like they don't care about me enough to even correctly write a short email. Try to ad a little humor and personality to your emails too. Don't just sound like a boring marketing robot.

Wrong Traffic

You could be attracting lots of traffic to your site but they aren't the type of people to buy your products. You need to make sure you get your landing page in front of the right audience.

Wrong Product

I've been guilty of this mistake many times. Some products look great to me. But for some reason, there just isn't any demand for them. Demand means what people will pay for. Just because people find a product interesting doesn't mean they will spend money on it. It's best to promote products that offer real, long term solutions to problems rather than just gimmicks.

Make sure you have evidence the product sells. A product in demand is much more likely to provide profit than something riskier. You can try out some completely new products eventually when you trust it could generate demand. However, when you are just starting out it's best to use only proven products.

Conclusion

You are now ready to start making money with affiliate marketing. If you are new to affiliate marketing and learned from this book then Please write a quick review on Amazon. I put a lot of time and effort in revealing my methods here and it's the kind thing to do.

No matter what affiliate programs you sign up for always keep trying. If you encounter any trouble then read this book again in case you missed any vital details.

Good luck.

Affiliate Marketing

How to Make $10,000+ Per Month With Your Own Online Business

Ryan Cash